My Days...
My Pictures

A Journal of My Drawings

My Days... My Pictures

A Journal of My Drawings

Created by Kathleen Lashier

P.O.Box 2543 • Dunnellon, FL 34430
1-800-554-1345
www.mymemoryjournals.com

Memory Journals for Special People

Grandma, Tell Me Your Memories

Grandpa, Tell Me Your Memories

Mom, Share Your Life With Me

Dad, Share Your Life With Me

To the Best of My Recollection

To My Dear Friend

My Days...My Pictures

My Days...My Writings

My Life...My Thoughts

Sisters

Mom, Tell Me One More Story...Your Story of Raising Me

Dad, Tell Me One More Story...Your Story of Raising Me

Distributed By:

507 Industrial Street
Waverly, IA 50677

Printed in the U.S.A.
by G&R Publishing Co.

ISBN-13: 978-1-56383-054-9
ISBN-10: 1-56383-054-X
Item #5055

To the Author/Illustrator –

This is <u>your</u> book.
On each page there is an idea for you to draw.
Draw it in <u>your own best way</u>!
Use crayons or pencils, not markers, to draw the pictures.

Sometimes you will see a line for a name or a word. If you need help,
ask someone to write the word or spell the word for you. Sometimes you
will get to tell a story, and let someone else write it down for you.
On other pages, you may want to write and spell your answers in your
own way. Even if you're the only one who can read it, that's OK because –

you're the author!

Someday, when you look back at these pictures and stories, you will be reminded
of how you felt and how the world looked through your young eyes.

The Owner and Author of this book is

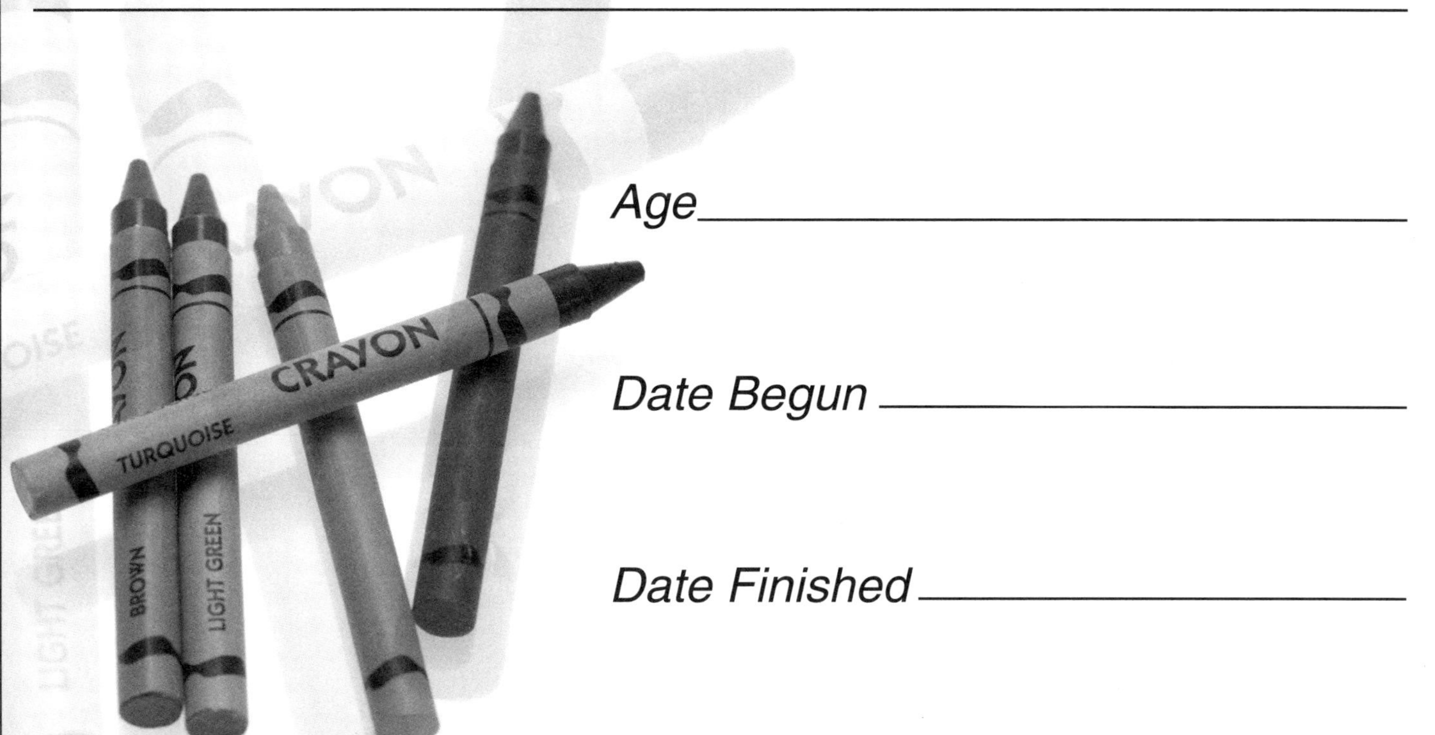

____

Age _______________________________

Date Begun _______________________________

Date Finished _______________________________

This book is dedicated
to all young authors,
and to the preservation of
their very important memories...

This is a picture of me.

My address is ________________________   *Today's date*________________

and my house looks like this.

I can draw a picture of my mom.   *Today's date*_______________

Her name is _______________________________.

My dad's name is ____________________________________ *Today's date*____________________

and he looks like this.

I'm learning to write my name like this.

I'm learning to write some numbers like this.

I was born on _______________________   *Today's date*_________________

and this is me, right after I was born.

Today ask your parents to write
a story about the day you were born.

*Today's date*______________

Today ask your mom or dad to write
about how they chose your first name...

*Today's date*__________________

...and your middle name.

I have _______ brothers
and _______ sisters and they look like this.

My phone # is

and the phone # for an emergency is

I draw a circle like this.

I draw a triangle like this.

I draw a square like this.

I draw a rectangle like this.

I'm learning to draw stars
and diamonds, but they are pretty hard!

*Today's date*_______________

This is my pet named _______________.

These are my favorite shoes.

Tell or Write

Today's date_______________________

I can make up a song about love. It goes like this…

My parents love it when I...

My parents don't like it when I…

These are my grandmas and grandpas.

My grandma's house looks like this…

When I am with my grandma, I like to...

When I am with my grandpa, I like to...

Tell or Write

Today's date_______________

List all the things you can think of that you love about having grandmas and grandpas.

This is my family's car.

My favorite thing to play with is…

In this space let your mom write what
she thinks is special about you.

*Today's date*__________________

In this space let your dad write what
he thinks is special about you.

Tell or Write

A rule we have at our house is…

We have that rule because…

I like it when my mom…

I like it when my dad…

This is my friend named _______________.

This is something that my friend and I like to do together.

My favorite home-cooked meal is

_______________________________ and looks like this.

Today's date_______________

In the winter, I wear these things to keep me warm.

This is a snowman that I
would like to have in my front yard.

*Today's date*___________________

This is something else
I like to do outside in the winter.

*Today's date*___________________

I can draw a pretty valentine like this.

One time I accidentally broke a...

Tell or Write

*Today's date*________________

My dad's job is __________________ and this is a drawing of what he does at work.

This is my dad's favorite thing to do
when he's not at work.

Tell or Write

*Today's date*______________

My mom's job is ________________________ and I can draw what she does at work.

This is my mom's favorite thing to do when she is not working.

*Today's date*___________________

I like to tell long stories, like this one:

> *Once upon a time, there was a very, very old man who...*

This is a picture of my story about the very, very old man.

My favorite movie is ___________________________,   *Today's date*___________________

and I can draw a picture from it…

Today ask your brother or sister to write
a note to you, or to draw a nice picture for you.

*Today's date*______________

This is the best present I ever gave to my mom.

This is the best present I ever gave to my dad.

If I went under the ocean,
this is what it would look like down there.

Today's date_______________

This is a place where I like to go out to eat _______________________________________, and this is what I like to eat there.

*Today's date*_________________

Ask your dad to write in this space about
what he did for fun when he was your age.

*Today's date*_______________

Ask your mom to write in this space about
what she did for fun when she was your age.

*Today's date*___________________

This is a bug that I see sometimes.

Tell, Write or Draw

Once I really fooled someone when I…

This is my very favorite thing I own.

Here are three things that Mom or Dad
would never let me bring into the house...

*Today's date*_______________

Around my yard we have birds that look like this...

The name of my school is __________________,   *Today's date*_______________

and it looks like this.

These are some of the kids
at my school and their names...

My teacher's name is ___________________,   *Today's date*___________________
and he/she looks like this.

This is something I do really well at school.

Today ask your <u>teacher</u> to write about
something that you are doing well at school.

*Today's date*__________________

When my teacher is happy, he/she says,

Tell or Write   *Today's date*________________

When my teacher is NOT happy, he/she says,

My favorite outfit to wear to school looks like this…

This is a picture of me playing
on my favorite playground equipment.

*Today's date*_________________

This is something I don't like
about going to school.

*Today's date*_______________

My yard at home looks like this.

The inside of my closet looks like this.

Of all the things I have,
the one that probably cost the most was…

*Today's date*_______________

My favorite sport to play is _____________________,   *Today's date*_________________
and this is how I do it.

I can draw a pretty butterfly.

Tell or Write

Today's date_______________

A special wish I have is…

Tell or Write

*Today's date*_______________

A special wish I have for someone ELSE is that…

I can draw a tree.

I am sometimes afraid of…

Tell or Write   *Today's date*___________________

Once when I was in a bad storm...

It looked like this.

I would like to have an umbrella that looks like this.

My favorite song or rhyme goes like this…

This is a picture of that favorite song or rhyme.

I can trace around my hand.

This is my favorite fruit.

This is my favorite vegetable.

This is a fun place I went with my family.

This is a picture of the biggest mistake I've ever made.

When my mom and dad go away,   *Today's date*__________________
I like it when __________________________ takes care of me.

This is something fun we do together.

Tell or Write   *Today's date*_____________

My favorite animal is a(n) _____________________ because…

and this is what it looks like.

This is what I want to do when I grow up.

Tell or Write

*Today's date*______________________

I will be good at that because…

I like to collect…

A famous person I would like to meet is

*Today's date*_________________

_______________________________ and he/she looks like this.

Sometimes I worry about…

At birthday parties it is fun to…

Tell or Write   *Today's date*________________

A bad habit that I have is…

This is a drawing of a GOOD habit that I have.

I can draw a pretty flower.

My favorite book is ________________________,   *Today's date*_______________
and it looks like this.

This is my Aunt _________________.

This is my Uncle ______________________________.

Tell, Write or Draw

Today's date_______________

Once I was really brave when…

Something that makes me really angry is   *Today's date*_______________

_____________________________, and I look like this.

This is my bedroom.

My favorite pajamas look like this.

When it's time for bed, I like to...

My favorite kind of sandwich is *Today's date*_____________

____________________________, and it looks like this.

This is the most dangerous thing a person can do.

When my dad is all dressed up, he is usually   *Today's date*__________________

going to ______________________________, and looks like this.

When my mom is all dressed up, she is usually   *Today's date*_______________
going to _______________________, and looks like this.

Today ask Mom or Dad to write a story
about something funny you once said or did.

This is my doctor and what he/she does.

This is my favorite stuffed animal
or doll named _______________________.

*Today's date*_______________

Today's date_______________

Three good rules parents should have for kids are:

1.

2.

3.

My favorite TV show is _____________________, *Today's date*_______________
and it looks like this.

Tell or Write

Today's date_______________

A police officer's job is to _______________________,
and this is how I draw it.

When I am sick, I like it when someone...

On the sidewalk, I like to ride around on my…

Today ask a baby-sitter to write
a funny story about you.

This is what our kitchen looks like.

I would like to go on a big trip to

___________________________, and it would look like this...

*Today's date*___________________

Tell, Write or Draw

My favorite thing to pretend is…

Tell or Write   *Today's date*___________________

The saddest thing that ever happened to me was when…

In the bathtub I like to…

The most beautiful thing I have ever seen was ___________________________, and it looked like this.

Today's date__________________

I can make up a good story about a dinosaur on this page...

...and draw a picture of it on the next page.

MY DINOSAUR PICTURE

My mom and I like to do this together…

My dad and I like to do this together…

This is my dentist...

and this is what he/she does to my teeth.

This is my cousin named ________________________.

Tell or Write

*Today's date*________________________

One thing that I would like to change about my life is…

This is something that really makes me laugh.

The country I live in is _________________,   *Today's date*_________________

and our country's flag looks like this.

The President of the United States is _____________________________ and he/she looks like this.

I saw a parade that looked like this.

In a swimming pool I like to…

This is something I like to do outside in the summer.

When I got hurt, this is how it happened…

The smartest thing I've ever done was…

Tell or Write

Today's date_______________

Trains are important because…

and they look like this.

I like to go to the park and do this…

Tell or Write

Today's date_______________

This is my favorite joke or riddle…

A pretty sunset looks like this.

I think every school should have a…

This is how I draw a rainbow…

At home, I am very good at…

Tell or Write

*Today's date*_________________

I would like to go to the moon because…

Three good rules teachers should have at school are:

1.

2.

3.

The principal at my school is probably
_____ years old and looks like this.

Tell or Write

Right now in school I am learning a lot about things like...

At recess I like to…

My most important job around the house is to…

I think heaven might look like this.

In my whole school, the person who is nicest to me   *Today's date*__________

is ________________, because ____________________,

and he/she looks like this.

The naughtiest thing I've ever done was…

The reason I did that was…

My favorite dessert looks like this.

I can draw a beautiful castle like this.

I think God looks like this.

Today ask Grandma or Grandpa or

*Today's date*_______________

Aunt or Uncle to write a poem or a limerick about you.

Some traffic signals I know look like this.

I would like to invent a funny machine
that looks like this.

This is what it would do.

If I had the neck of a giraffe I could

_______________________________, and this is how it would look...

*Today's date*_________________

On my birthday I like to…

This is a picture of a birthday cake I had.

One of my birthday presents this year was _______________________, and it looks like this.

*Today's date*_______________

Tell, Write or Draw.

Today's date_________________

A very nice thing that I could do for someone right now would be...

If these holiday pages do not pertain to your family, you can remove this section or change the questions to reflect your holidays and traditions.

We celebrate Easter every spring because…

and this is what we do.

This is what I like to do on the 4th of July.

We have fun at Halloween when we…

Once I wore a costume that looked like this.

Tell or Write

Today's date________________

We celebrate Thanksgiving every fall because…

and this is what we do.

I am thankful for…

I think a pilgrim looked like this…

We celebrate Christmas every winter because…

and this is what we do.

I think Santa Claus looks like this.

This is how Santa Claus gets around.

My Christmas tree usually looks like this.

At Christmas I really like to…

This year
I would like to give Mom a…

*Today's date*________________

I would like to give Dad a…

Tell or Write

*Today's date*_______________

List all the things your mom does that make her a great mom.

Tell or Write

Today's date___________________

List all the things your dad does that make him a great dad.

You are now the author AND illustrator of your very own book! Congratulations!

Today's date________________

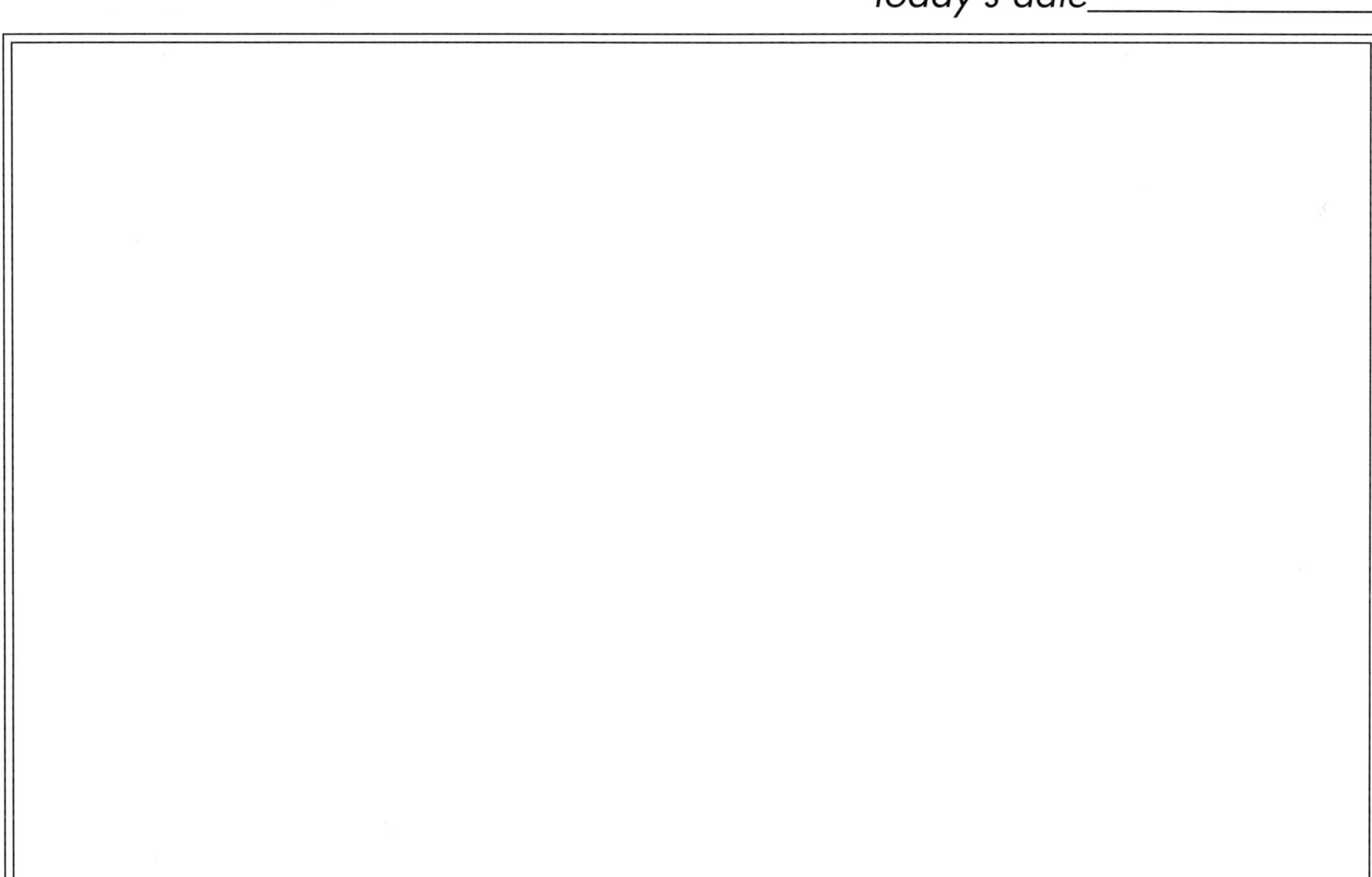

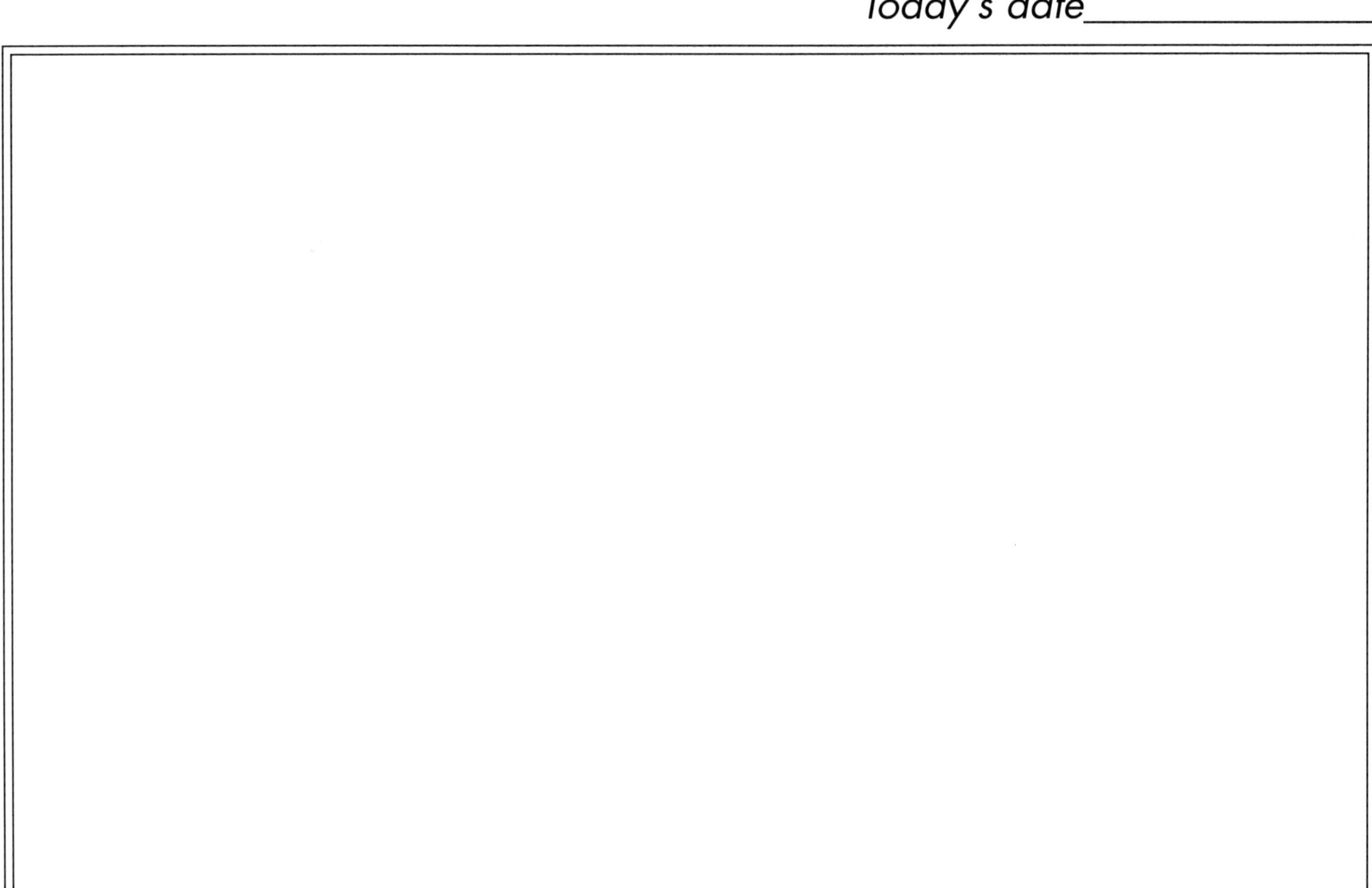

Today's date__________________

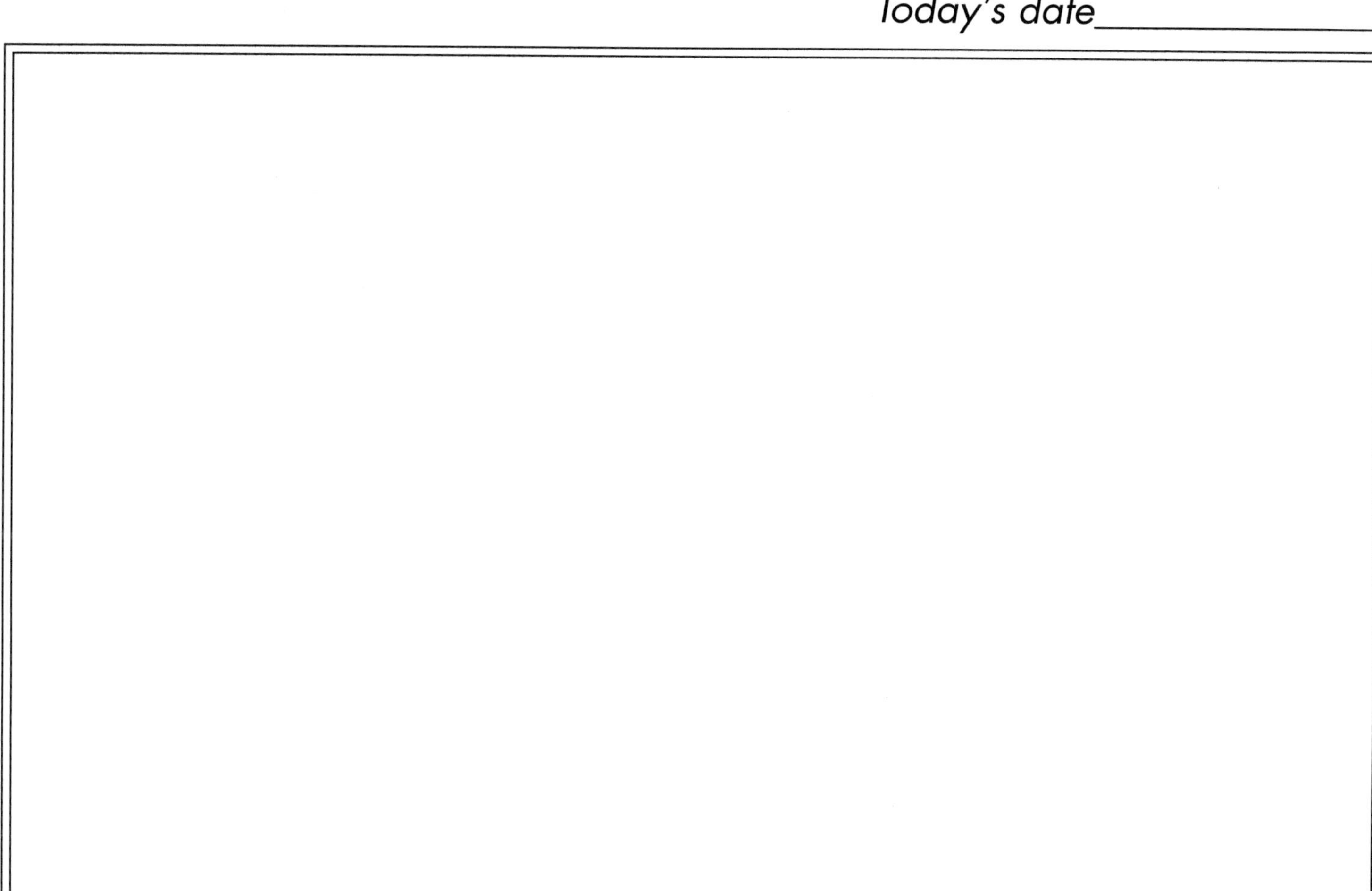

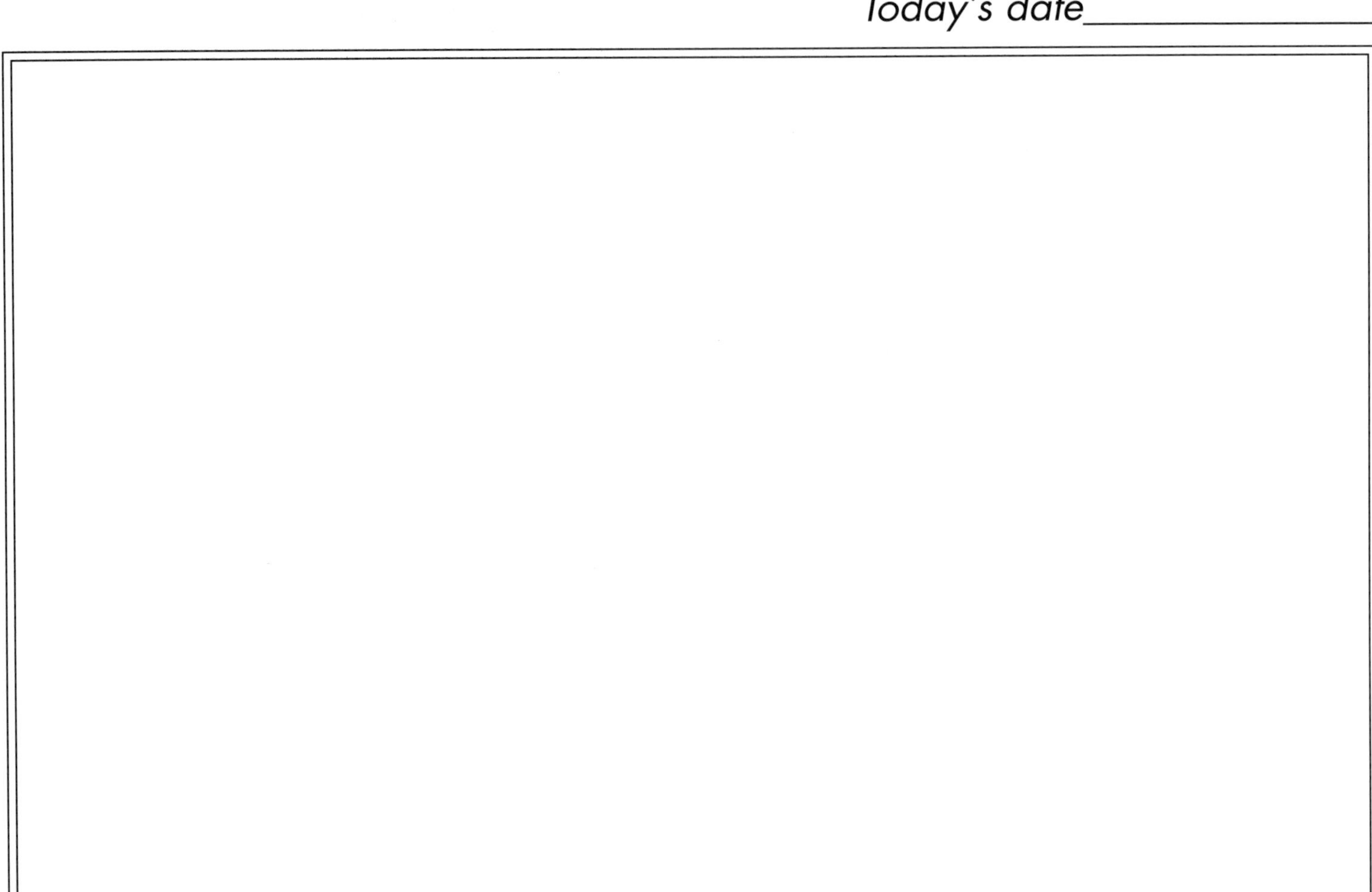

Today's date

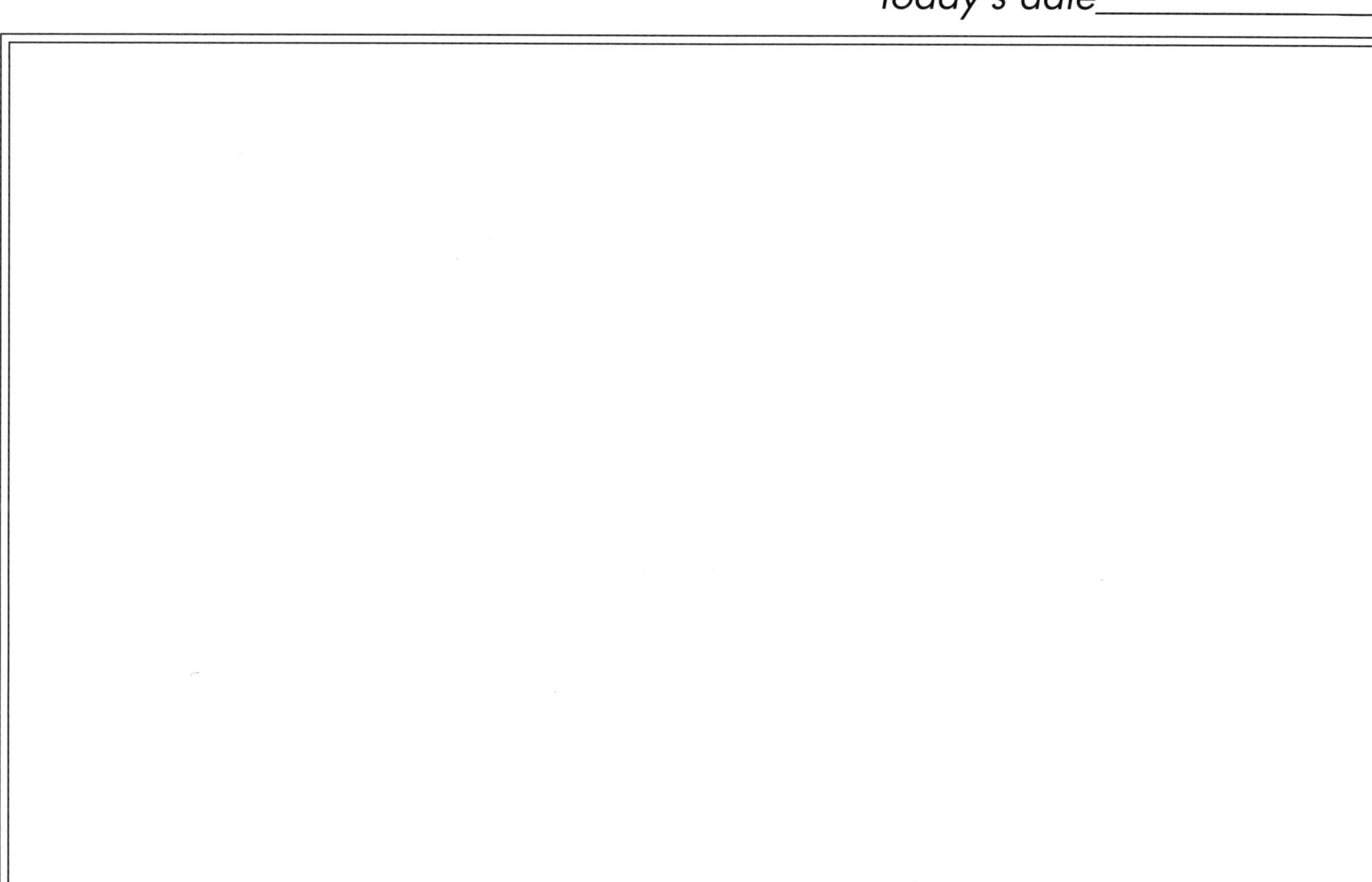

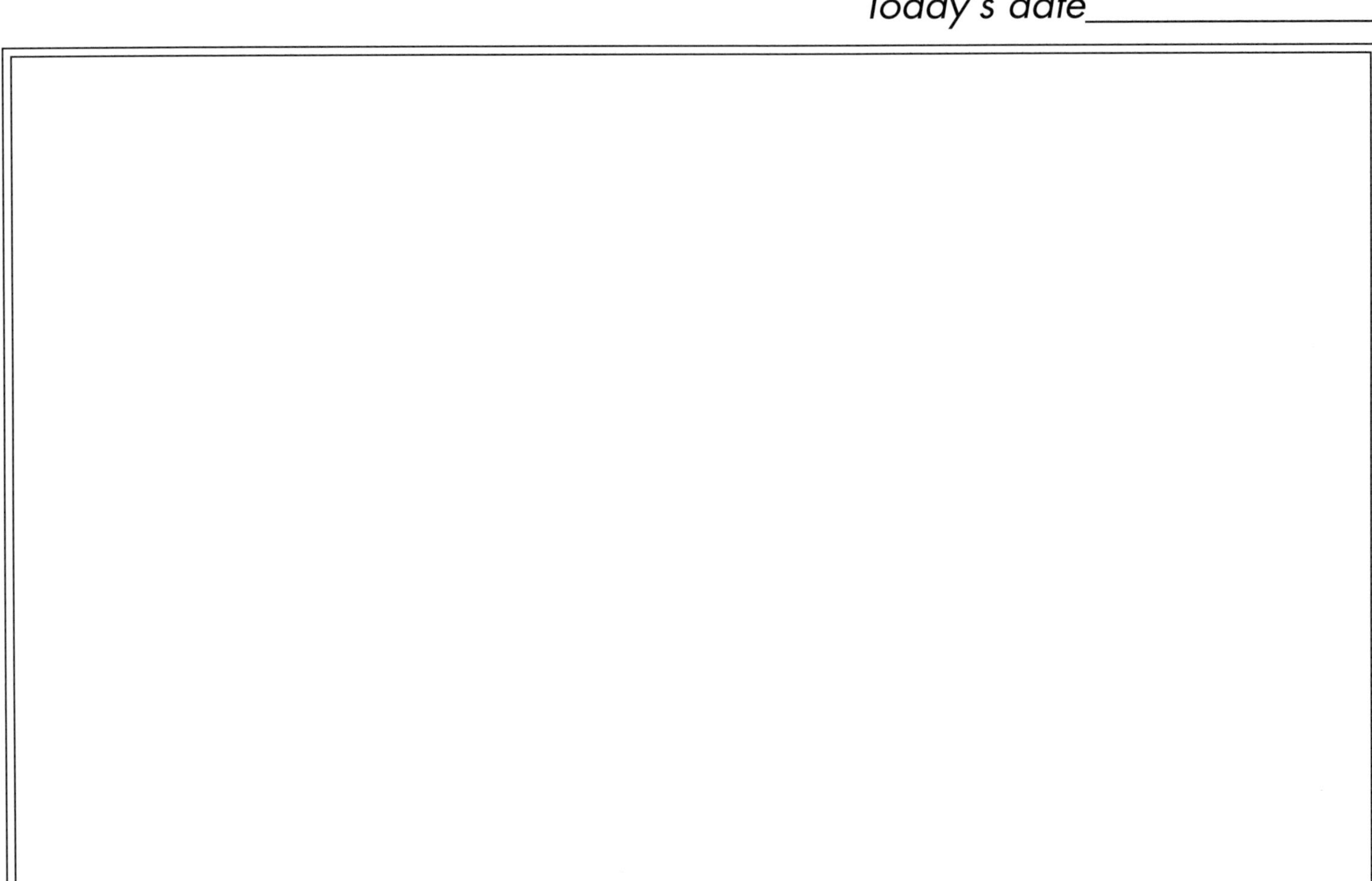

Today's date_______________

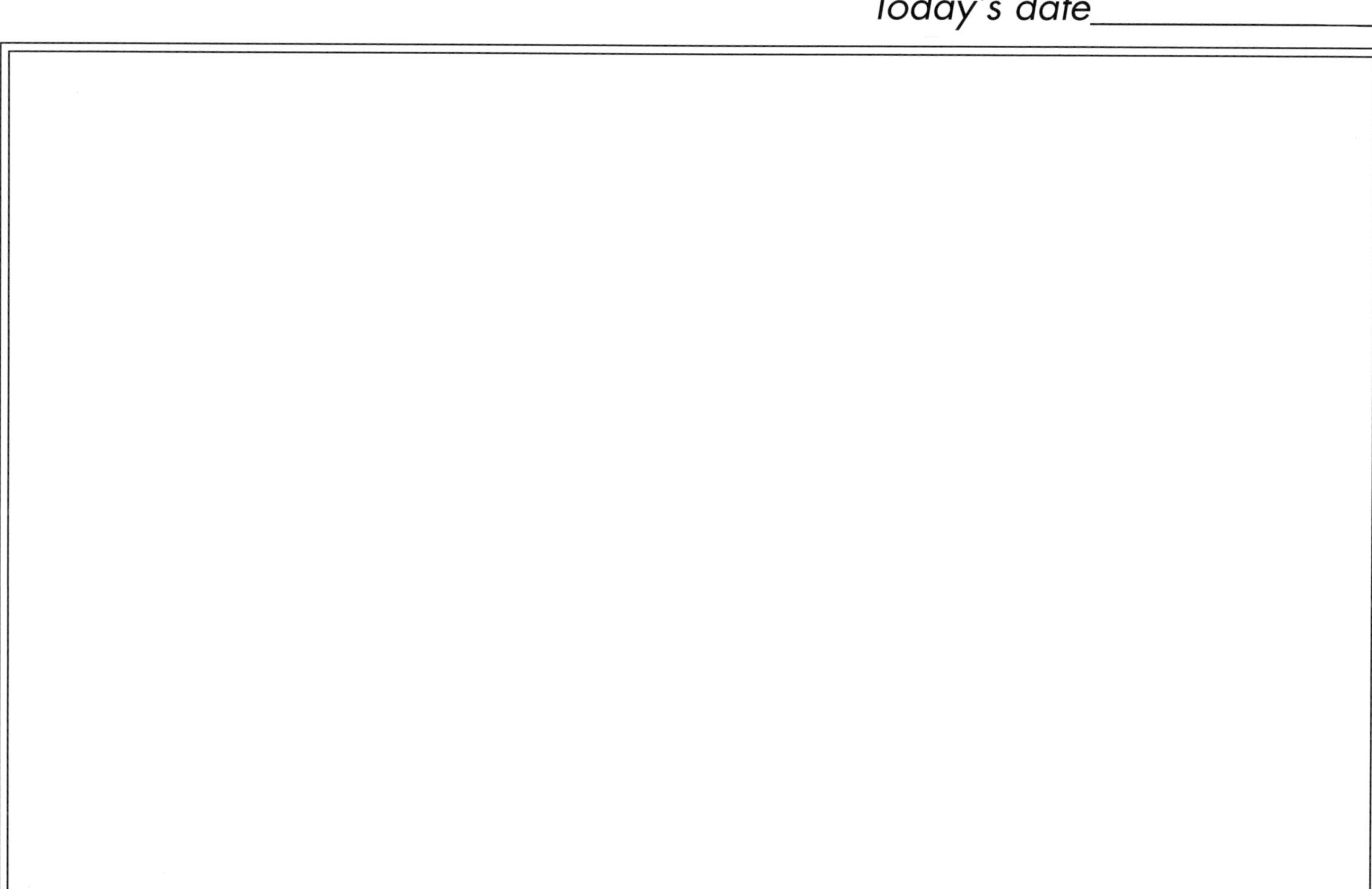

Today's date______________________

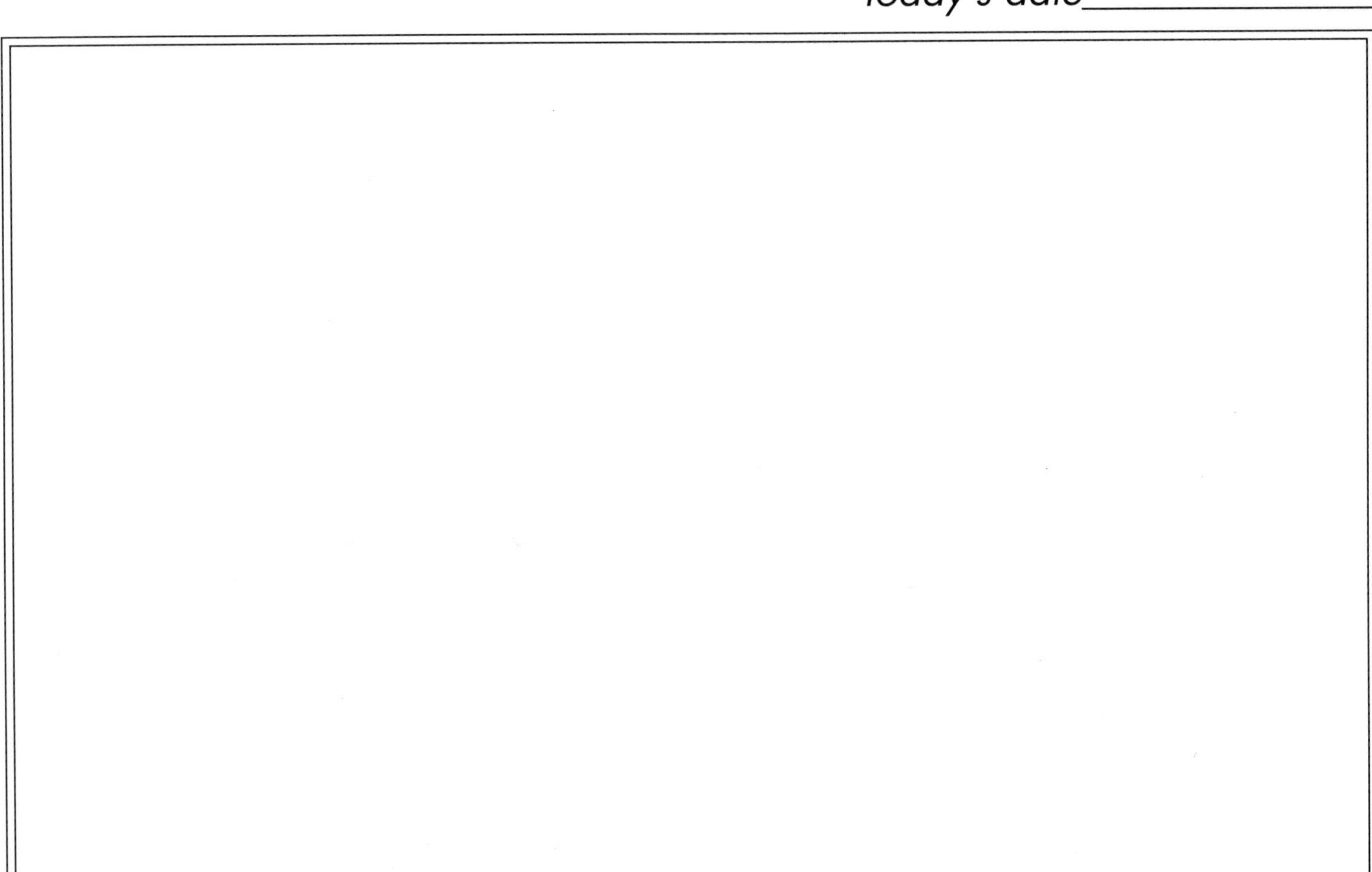

Today's date________________

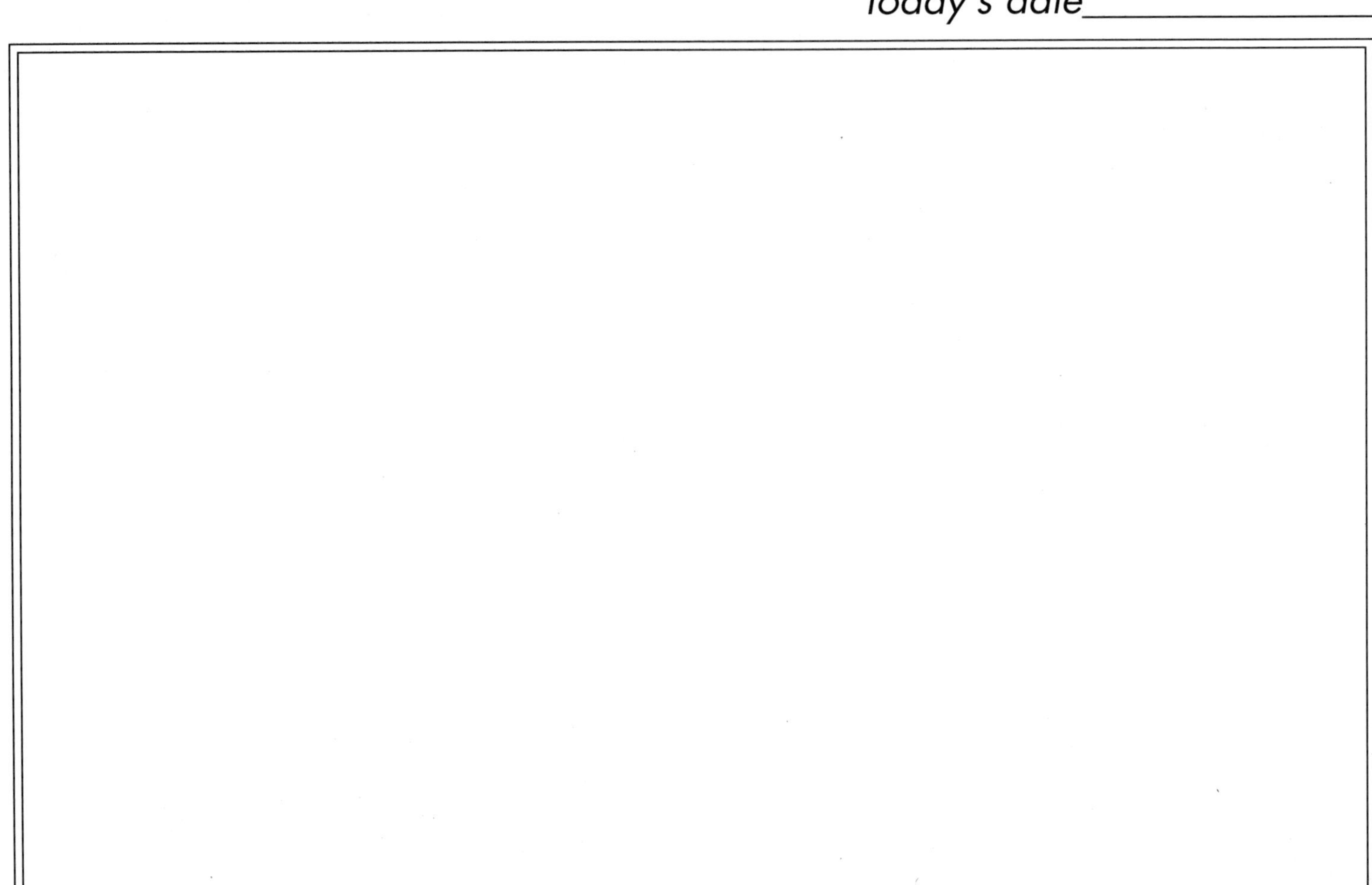